Marissa —
Merry Christmas
1982
to our <u>favorite</u>
dancer!
Love, Aunt Lynn & Uncle Bill

A Very Young Dancer

A so By Jill Krementz

The Face of South Vietnam
(with text by Dean Brelis)

Sweet Pea—A Black Girl
Growing Up in the Rural South

Words and Their Masters
(with text by Israel Shenker)

A Very Young Rider

A Very Young Gymnast

A Very Young Circus Flyer

A Very Young Skater

How It Feels When a Parent Dies

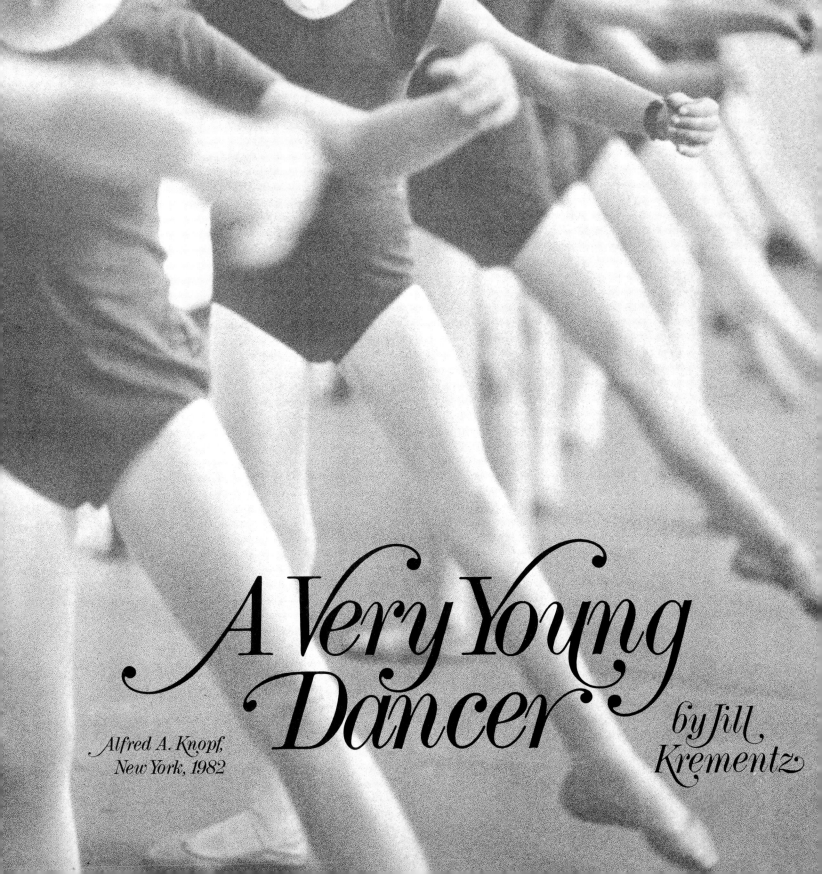

A Very Young Dancer

by Jill Krementz

Alfred A. Knopf,
New York, 1982

This is a Borzoi Book
published by Alfred A. Knopf, Inc.
Copyright © 1976 by Jill Krementz
All rights reserved under International and Pan-American Copyright Conventions.
Published in the United States by Alfred A. Knopf, Inc., New York, and
simultaneously in Canada by Random House of Canada Limited, Toronto.
Distributed by Random House, Inc., New York.
Library of Congress Catalog Card Number: 76-13700
ISBN: 0-394-40885-3
Manufactured in the United States of America
Published November 9, 1976
Reprinted Twelve Times
Fourteenth Printing, March 1982
Graphics were directed by R. D. Scudellari, and Elissa Ichiyasu assisted
in the design and layout of the book.

The author is donating a portion of her proceeds from this book to The School of American Ballet.

For Kurt, with love

I don't know if I want to be a dancer when I grow up—or if I want to do something with horses. I really like horses. I have a pony in Wyoming where we go for the whole summer. It's near Yellowstone Park. My pony's name is Rosetta. My name is Stephanie.

I love ballet too. I've been taking lessons since I was six. I'm ten now. My sister Andrea, who is twelve, started when she was eight. We both go to The School of American Ballet. She's taking toe this year and she lets me try on her slippers. Next year I'll take toe for five minutes at the end of each class. Andrea says it makes you feel big but that's just in the beginning. After a while it just hurts. You get blisters and bunions. Her feet are a mess. You should see them.

Mommy used to dance. She once choreographed her own ballet. If I have a problem, she helps me. Last year she came to class and made some notes about which things I could do better. The parents all get to visit one day in April.

Mr. George Balanchine is the head of the New York City Ballet. The School of American Ballet was started by a friend of his named Lincoln Kirstein because Mr. Balanchine wanted a place where he could train dancers to do the kind of dancing he likes. It's in the same building as the Juilliard School of Music in New York. They teach boys there too, but mostly girls. You have to audition to get in and it's very strict. I was eight when I tried out. I had already studied for two years with a teacher named Anita Zahn.

As soon as we get to school we change into our leotards and tights. The school is divided into eleven divisions, starting with the first and going up to the most advanced class, which is for any age. Each division has a different color leotard. I'm in third division and wear hemlock green. We all have to wear pink tights. I have three classes a week: Tuesdays and Thursdays at four and Saturday mornings at half-past nine. Andrea's in fifth division and has five classes a week.

Tina and I have our lockers next to each other. She's my best friend.

If you have long hair, you have to wear it up so the teacher can be sure your neck and shoulders look right. I'm not very good at doing it myself so Andrea usually helps me in the car on the way over.

On weekdays we come from regular school so we have to rush to get ready. If we're late they get really mad and sometimes we aren't allowed to take class if we don't have a good excuse.

Sometimes we rush so much that we get to the studio early and so we sit and watch the older girls until it's time.

Edith Hogsett takes attendance. She's been at the school for twelve years. There are twenty-eight in my class when nobody is absent, but that hardly ever happens. Dancers are always hurting themselves. If we miss a lot of classes it's very hard to catch up and make it into the next division.

We start every class working at the barre. We're arranged according to height and I'm third on the barre. When you're in the advanced division you get to stand any place you want.

I've heard that if you don't reach five feet three inches by a certain age you have to leave the school.

We have different piano players and some of them, like Frida, are from Russia and played for ballet schools there.

Work at the barre really gets boring sometimes, but Carol Sumner, who's one of our teachers, tells us that if we're bored it means we're not doing it right. She studied ballet at this school when she was little and Mr. Balanchine made her a dancer in the company when she was only eighteen. She's a soloist now. She and Patricia McBride were in the same division.

David Richardson teaches us sometimes and he's in the company too. He's always telling me to pull in my stomach. On Saturdays we have Miss Reiman. She used to be a dancer for Mr. Balanchine and she's been in movies but I've never seen them. My favorite movies are *Mary Poppins*, *Bedknobs and Broomsticks*, and *The Sound of Music*. I liked *Benji* too.

Sometimes we do demi-pointe.

We always do tendus.

Each teacher has a different routine for us, but most of the exercises are the same. They're just in a different order. The names of the steps are all in French because the first national ballet school was in France. We work at the barre for about an hour. You have to do this to get your muscles all warmed up so you can jump. Even the company dancers do this before they perform.

I don't mind the barre exercises except I don't like rond de jambe en l'air because it's too tiring and it hurts my leg. But it doesn't hurt everybody's leg. Carol Sumner makes us do it fast and it doesn't hurt so much then.

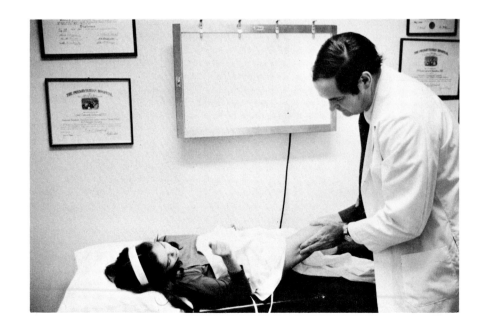

Once I hurt my leg so much I had to see Dr. Hamilton. He's the company doctor. He took some X-rays and told me that I couldn't take class for a month.

When we finish at the barre we all go into the center of the room and the teacher has us do different things.

We're not supposed to talk but sometimes Tina and I do anyway.

I like the jumping best of all and Michelle, Tina, and I try to jump together.

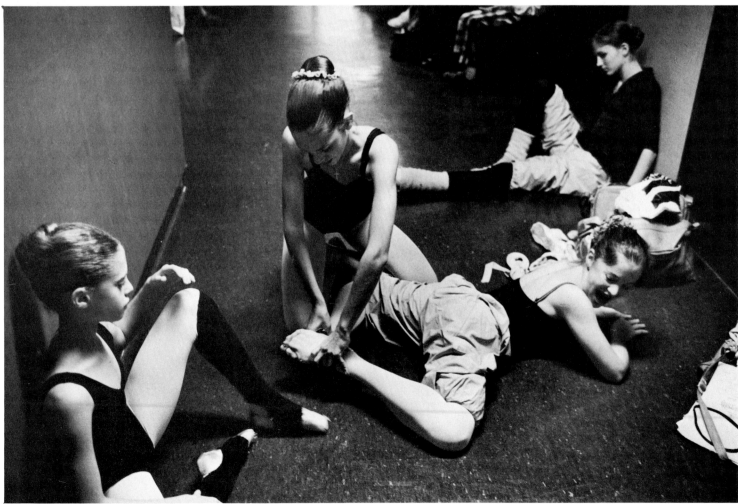

When we come out of the studio the halls are always full of the older girls. They limber up before class. Sometimes they wear rubber pants over their leotards to get their muscles really warm. They have to take them off before class though.

After I change out of my leotard, I usually check the bulletin board to see if there are any announcements. And then I go downstairs and find Mommy, who's waiting in the car to take me home. She always asks me if I have a lot of homework and I always tell her yes. On the night that Andrea stays late for toe class, Mommy has to make two trips.

They give us so much homework at our school that it's really hard for me to get it done on the nights I've been to ballet class.

Sometimes, when I don't have too much homework, I like to go to the ballet itself. My favorite ballet is *Coppélia,* and this year Andrea was in it. She was in "The Waltz of the Golden Hours" and got to wear a pretty pink tutu.

Patricia McBride often dances the lead in *Coppélia* and she's one of my favorite dancers. It's a hard part because she has so much to do. I like it when she pretends she's the doll.

Peter Martins is also one of my favorite dancers. He danced the lead male role in *Coppélia* this year quite a few times. He's so light on his feet. I mean, he's muscular but he doesn't thump on the floor. We see him a lot over at school because he likes to take classes with Stanley Williams, who is one of the teachers there.

Afterwards I go backstage and tell Andrea how good she was. I see lots of other people I know too: David, my teacher, who plays the part of the Mayor; Mischa Arshansky, who did my makeup when I was in *A Midsummer Night's Dream;* and Charlotte and Catherine d'Amboise, whose father is in the company. They're twins but I don't think they look alike at all. I also talk with Nina Fedorova. She and her sister used to baby-sit for me and Andrea. Lots of girls in the company do baby-sitting to earn a little extra money.

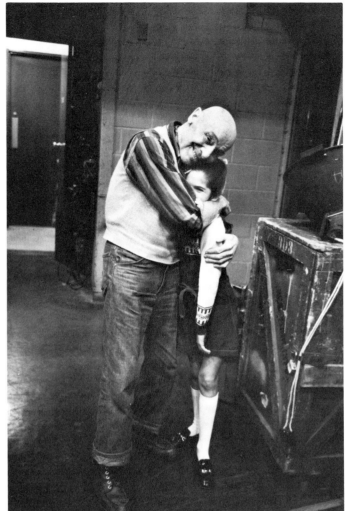

One of the good things about going to The School of American Ballet is that you get to be in a lot of the real ballets because Mr. Balanchine uses a lot of children. They even pay you. It's about $7.50 a performance. I had to get a Social Security number. They send you a check and I put mine in the bank.

I've been in *Circus Polka, The Nutcracker, A Midsummer Night's Dream,* and *L'Enfant et les Sortilèges. Nutcracker* and *Circus Polka* were my favorites. Igor Stravinsky wrote *Circus Polka* for real elephants and Mr. Balanchine went down to Florida to the Barnum and Bailey Circus and choreographed it there. All the elephants wore pink tutus and pink ribbons in their hair—all except for the head elephant, who wore a blue tutu and a blue ribbon. Vera Zorina, who was one of Mr. Balanchine's most famous ballerinas, rode on top of the elephant in blue on opening night. When they did the ballet in New York, Jerome Robbins did the choreography. He used thirty-nine of the youngest children from the school instead of real elephants. Mr. Robbins was the ringmaster and I was the naughty elephant. It was my first ballet and it was so much fun.

In *L'Enfant et les Sortilèges,* Andrea and I were both toads with lots of big warts. All we had to do was hop around. It was the easiest ballet I've ever been in.

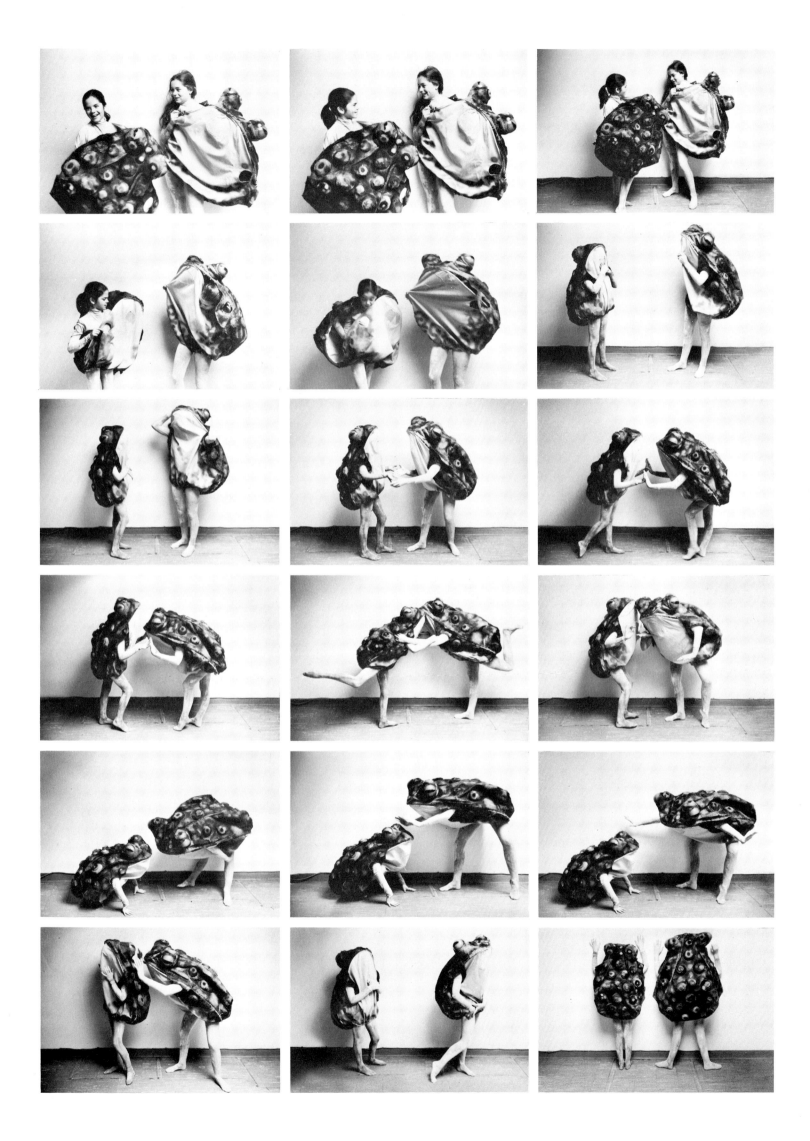

I guess *Nutcracker* is the most exciting of all because it runs for so many performances. The music for *Nutcracker*, which is based on a Hoffmann fairy tale, was written by Tchaikovsky. It's about a little girl named Mary who gets a wooden nutcracker for Christmas. It turns into a prince and takes Mary to the Land of Sweets, and they live happily ever after.

Last year I was in the party scene in the first act and I was an angel in Act II. Andrea was in *Nutcracker* three years in a row. It's the only ballet you have to audition for, and practically everyone in the school tries out. For the other ballets you just get picked.

David Richardson puts an announcement on the bulletin board giving the date and the time for *Nutcracker* auditions. They are always on a Saturday afternoon. This year they were on the Saturday after Halloween.

Everyone wants to have their hair looking nice for the audition so Mommy came to do mine. David likes you to have your hair down so he can see how long it is.

Tina, Michelle, and I waited outside together while David talked to the mothers. He told them not to be upset or pester him if their children weren't picked. I was really scared. Tina, Michelle, and I all wanted to get the party scene. Tina was the bunny last year.

Finally David opened the door and told us to come in. We all stood around him and he told us that if we weren't picked it didn't necessarily mean we weren't good. It just meant that either we were too tall or our legs weren't strong enough.

Then he told us to sit around the room and wait for him to call our division.

Some people auditioned in groups and some by themselves, depending on which parts they were trying out for. David demonstrated a step for the Polichinelles' dance in Act II. They're the ones who come out from under Mother Ginger's skirt. Everybody wants to be in that because they do the most dancing but he only needs sixteen—eight for each cast. There's an A Cast and a B Cast for the children and they take turns doing the performances. About eighty-two children get to be in *Nutcracker*.

Some of the grown-up dancers came to watch the auditions, like Karin von Aroldingen and Kay Mazzo. And there were some newspaper reporters. The mothers weren't allowed in, but a lot of them waited outside in the hall.

Finally it was my turn. David asked me to do an emboité.

I was so scared, and when I'm scared I always think I won't get picked.

After everyone had auditioned, David started picking people. First he picked all the party scene parts and then he walked over and picked me and Susie Eisner for the part of Mary. I couldn't believe it!

Then David picked all the other parts—the angels, mice, soldiers, hoops, Polichinelles, and the bunny. Tina got picked for the bunny again and felt very sad because she wanted to be in the party scene so much. I told her she should be happy because it meant that David thought she did such a good job last year. We'll both be in B Cast. She'll also be an angel in Act II. Almost everyone who gets picked does two parts.

After all the parts were chosen, the press photographers asked Susie and me to pose with our princes. Stephen Austin was picked for Cast B with me and Sean Savoye for Cast A. Sean was Susie's prince last year too. He broke his wrist in class when another dancer kicked him with a piqué en arabesque by mistake.

When you're in *Nutcracker,* or in any ballet, you get free shoes from the company. Most of us go to Capezio. For the first act party scene I wear black shoes, and then I change to white. So I got two pairs.

The elastics come separately and you have to sew them on yourself. Mommy sews them on for me. The older dancers are always sewing their slippers. I wear size 2.

After I got fitted for my shoes, I went to Madame Pourmel to get measured for my costume. She's the head wardrobe lady. They have a few dresses for Mary but none of them fit me so everyone decided Madame Karinska should make me a new one.

Andrea is always very careful about what she eats, but I'm not very good at it. Sometimes I go on little diets—like I don't eat liver or brussels sprouts.

David was in charge of teaching all the children their parts. He gave us schedules and we had to come to the rehearsal studios at the New York State Theater. That's where the New York City Ballet has its performances and also where the company dancers take their classes. It's about two blocks away from the school, so we can just run over after our regular dance classes. Sometimes I had to eat a quick dinner between class and rehearsal.

I had about five rehearsals a week and each one lasted an hour. My first few rehearsals were for me alone, and David showed me how to do the running when the Christmas tree starts growing and the mice are chasing me. He said I had to run very fast and that I mustn't make any noise. He told me that the most important thing about dancing was to make it look as natural as possible and that running and walking are the hardest things to do on stage. I agree.

After three or four rehearsals by myself, I rehearsed with Stephen. We did the part at the end of Act I when I'm lying in bed and he comes in with the crown and kisses my hand. Stephen wasn't half as embarrassed as I was.

Stephen is a year older than me and studies ballet with his own teacher a few times a week. He and his brother, Michael, have been in quite a lot of ballets and Michael was my partner last year for the "Grandfather's Dance" in the party scene.

David Richardson, my teacher, played the part of the prince for Mr. Balanchine when he was thirteen. And Mr. B. also played the part of the prince, when he was young and still living in Russia.

Then we worked on the part where Stephen puts the crown on my head and we walk off the stage together.

David told me I should keep my stomach in and stand up like a princess…that I have to be very grand for that walk up the center of the stage. He told me to ask Susie Eisner how to fix my hair so the crown wouldn't fall off.

We really had to work on the part where the Nutcracker fights the Mouse King and I throw my slipper.

The first time I hit Stephen by mistake but then I hit David and I was so happy.

In some of the rehearsals we worked on the soldier scene. All the soldiers and the bunny, which is Tina, help the Nutcracker to fight off the mice.

Stephen got to practice with a sword. David told me I had to act very scared while the Nutcracker was having his duel.

We had a lot of rehearsals for the party scene, which is in the beginning when all the children come to my house on Christmas Eve and we all get presents. It's when I get the nutcracker and all the children dance.

The "Grandfather's Dance" was the only dance I knew because I did it last year.

During the last week of rehearsals we practiced some scenes with the dancers in the company. I worked with the big mice on the parts where they scare me and I have to jump into the air.

And Stephen did his sword fight with Paul Sackett, who plays the Mouse King some of the time. Tina had to pull his tail. He wasn't in costume so she just had to pretend. All the grown-up parts are played by lots of different dancers.

Except for Drosselmeyer. He is always played by Shaun O'Brien, who has been in *Nutcracker* for twenty-two years. That is how long *Nutcracker* has been performed at the New York City Ballet. For the past few years he's done every performance. He's a really good actor, and he's never sick. I can't believe it. We rehearsed the whole beginning of Act I where he arrives with all the presents and his nephew, who is Stephen. It's Drosselmeyer who gives me the nutcracker as a Christmas present. He's sort of like a magician.

At one of our last rehearsals I had to do the opening scene of Act I when I'm sitting in front of the curtain with my brother Fritz. Adam Holland plays that part. There are only two other boys besides him and Stephen in our cast of *Nutcracker*. All the other boys' parts are played by girls.

Finally we went up for a rehearsal with Mr. Balanchine in the big dance studio where he teaches class to the company dancers every morning. Everyone from both casts was there—all the children and the entire company. It was the first time we rehearsed with the Sugar Plum Fairy, mostly with Colleen Neary since it was her first year too—as Sugar Plum, that is. She's been the Dew Drop Fairy before.

I was a little bit scared because there were so many people watching, including Mr. Balanchine and his assistant, Rosemary Dunleavy.

On the day before opening I took the day off from school because we had so many rehearsals and because I had to go to Madame Karinska's costume shop to try on my new dress. I gave her a little heart-shaped box as a present. She took me into the fitting room and tried on my new costume. She made me lift my arms up to see if I could move around O.K. and it was fine.

She's eighty-nine years old and has been making costumes for Mr. B. for thirty years. She once won an Oscar for her costumes for a movie about Joan of Arc.

After the fitting Mommy and I went into her office and she showed us some Audubon prints. She is designing costumes for a future ballet of Mr. Balanchine's which might be called *Birds of America*. She gave me some handmade lace and kissed me goodbye. She's nice. She told me that one time she played the part of the Grandmother in *Nutcracker* because Mr. Balanchine asked her to.

We had two dress rehearsals, one for Act I and another for Act II. I talked backstage with Patricia McBride, who plays the part of the Sugar Plum Fairy some of the time. She was warming up at the barre in her leg warmers.

The children all wore their costumes but some of the older dancers didn't. Drossel-meyer just wore his bathrobe and the mice didn't bother with their mouse heads.

Stephen said the good thing about wearing the nutcracker head is that he can count all the time to the music and not worry about the audience seeing him.

Mr. B. showed Tina how to turn after she pulls the mouse's tail. He told her she should pull it, jump, and then run and look back.

Then he came over to the bed and showed me how to faint. It's much harder than it looks because you have to fall backward a certain way.

Later that day, we got ready to rehearse Act II. One thing Mr. B. is very particular about is how everyone's costume looks and fits.

Mostly we practiced the part where Stephen and I leave the Land of Sweets.

And then all the rehearsing was over. We were ready to open.

Our cast opened on a Saturday matinee and I started getting ready around noon.
Andrea did my makeup at home.

Just before I left for the theater I got some flowers from Grammy. And a close
friend of ours sent me a little basket with nuts and crackers for *Nutcracker.*

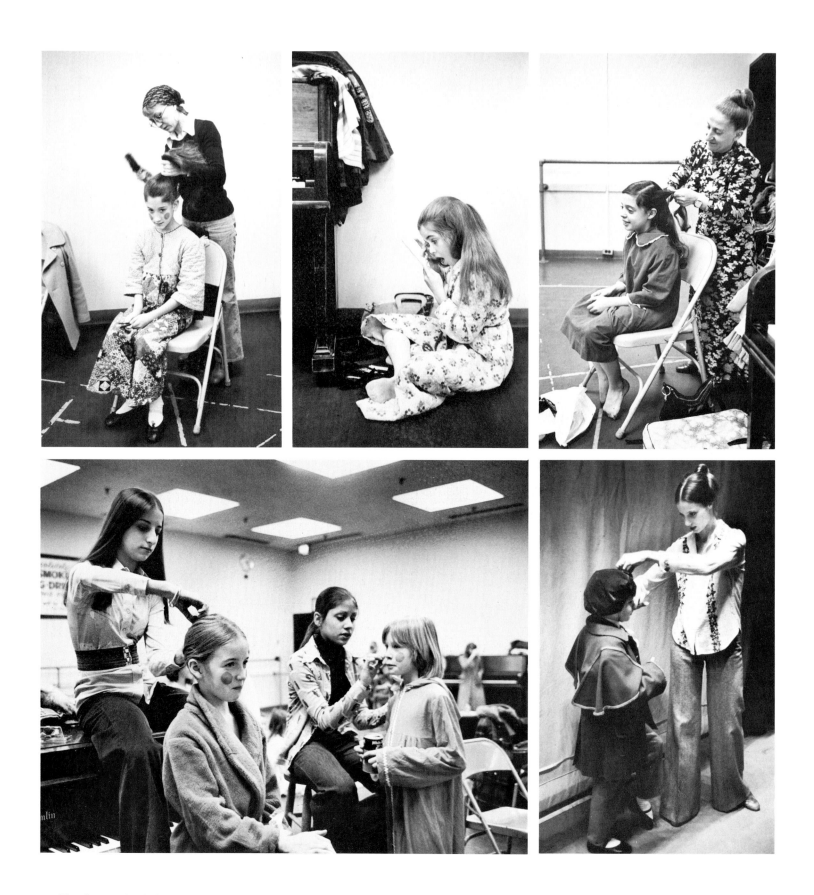

All the children, the girls that is, fix their hair and makeup in one big room two floors below the stage. Some mothers help out, and so do Pam and Regina, who are advanced students at the school. The boys get dressed down on the fourth floor. Kenny Mineker got special help from his aunt who is Suzanne Farrell. She wasn't dancing that afternoon so she came to watch him in the party scene. Suzanne was an angel in *Nutcracker* when she was a student. She's a principal dancer with the New York City Ballet now.

Then we go up one flight to wardrobe, in shifts, depending on which part we have, to get into our costumes. The party scene is first, then soldiers, angels, Polichinelles, and hoops. Désirée dressed me.

After we were all dressed for the party scene we waited for the stage manager to call us. They call three times. First to say "Fifteen minutes," then "Five minutes," and then . . . "On stage."

Finally the phone rang for the third time and I answered it, saying "Wardrobe."
Ronnie Bates was saying "On stage, please. On stage for Act I." I said "Thank
you," and we all ran for the elevator.

Mommy wished me good luck. The one thing Mommy never says is "Break a leg," which is supposed to be good luck, but I'm not sure Mommy thinks so.

Everybody came. Grammy, Daddy, my brother Christopher, and Andrea.

The first thing I did was to put my brush on the white bed because I have a quick change of clothes between scenes in the first act, and I have to fix my hair.

Carolyn Loudon showed me how to get a better grip on the nutcracker because my hand wasn't big enough to hold it the way David told me to. She played the part of Mary in Saratoga last year.

Then John Walters told me to sit in the chair for the opening scene with Fritz kneeling beside me, and they lowered the scrim curtain behind me. I could hear the musicians playing the overture but I couldn't see anything and we waited in the dark for the curtain to go up. I was a little nervous but once the curtain went up I wasn't scared because all I was thinking about was doing the right things and not forgetting what David had told me to do.

I had to have my eyes closed and I was counting the notes so I would wake up at the right time. When I opened my eyes I could see Robert Irving, the conductor. He smiled at me.

Then all the guests start arriving and the party scene begins. The scrim curtain goes up and there's a beautiful Christmas tree behind it. Drosselmeyer and his nephew show up with all their presents. I got a good grip on the nutcracker, thanks to Carolyn, and Fritz got through the smashing scene without really wrecking it. Roland, the assistant stage manager, showed Adam a special way to throw the nutcracker on the floor so it wouldn't break.

We did the part where we're rocking our dolls, and then the "Grandfather's Dance." Everyone clapped after we did the dance and then the party scene was over. I felt silly when Stephen and I had to hold hands.

During the next scene I am on stage all alone. I have to pick up the nutcracker from its little bed and get on the sofa with it and fall asleep. Drosselmeyer tiptoes in while I'm sleeping and fixes the nutcracker so it doesn't have to have a bandage anymore. My arm really felt squished because of the way I had to lie down.

And then it was my favorite scene. That's when the mice appear in my dream along with the soldiers and the tree starts to grow. Tina told me that she would smile at me if I was doing good and if I was bad she would frown. That afternoon she forgot to do anything, but I smiled at her. It was nice to be on stage together. Some of the mice stepped on my feet and it was hard not to step on their tails.

When the tree starts growing it's the most exciting thing. It gets gigantic! It's the scene I remember most from all the times I saw *Nutcracker* before I was in it.

Everything starts to grow—even the nutcracker in its tiny bed. It's very scary!

The soldiers and the mice have a big fight and I wake up the Nutcracker, who is now Stephen, so he can help the soldiers.

I just watch until the battle is over and the huge mice carry off the soldiers.

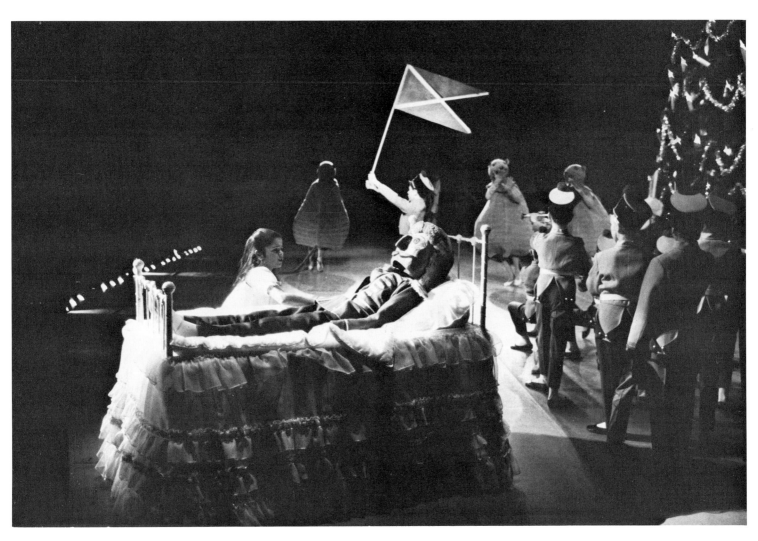

Then Stephen has his duel with the Mouse King and I throw my slipper.

I missed and my shoe almost went into the orchestra pit.

The Mouse King chases me back to the bed and that's when I faint and Stephen stabs him with his sword. He cuts off one of the Mouse King's golden crowns and brings it to me. When he put it on my head it was so wobbly I was sure it was going to fall off, but it didn't. You have to get the comb in just right and we didn't have enough time to practice. David told me that if my crown ever does fall off, I should pick it up and carry it in front of me. The snow tickled when it went inside my nightgown.

When we walk off toward the star, that's the end of Act I and the curtain comes down. In ballet they have curtain calls after every act and whoever had big solo parts in that act takes special bows. Drosselmeyer, Stephen, and I took our special bows together. Stephen sent me a bouquet of flowers, which was presented to me on stage. They were so pretty.

As soon as the curtain calls are over, we have a half-hour intermission. The stage-hands have to clean up all the snow and change the scenery for Act II. The scenery is so beautiful. It was designed by Rouben Ter-Arutunian, who designs lots of the sets and costumes for the New York City Ballet. He did *Coppélia* too.

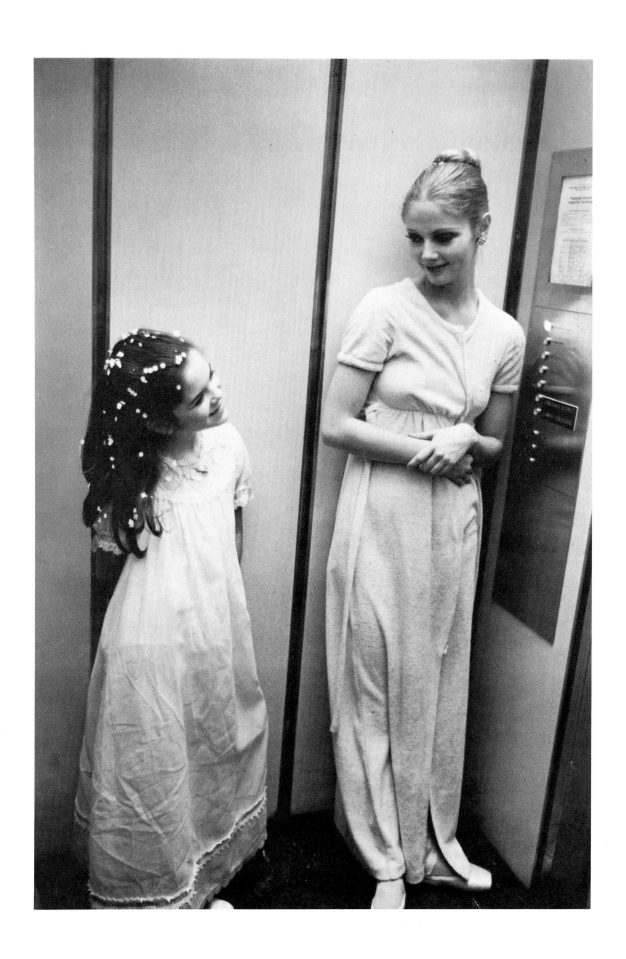

I went down to the wardrobe room in the elevator with Judy Fugate, who is one of the dancers in the company and was one of the parents in the party scene. She played the part of Mary when she was only seven and did the part for four years.

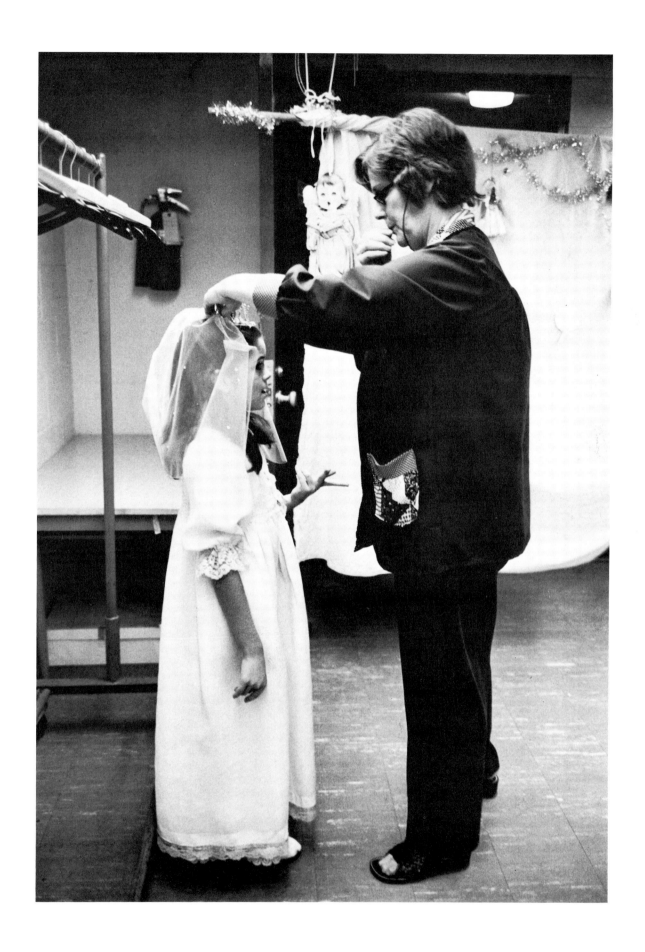

Her mother is the wardrobe mistress and is in charge of getting me ready for Act II, when I have to wear a crown and a veil. I think it looks as though I'm getting married, but it's really because I'm a princess.

It only takes a few minutes to fix my costume so I went right back to the stage to watch everyone warming up for Act II. I checked my crown to be sure it looked O.K. and then Tina and I waited on stage. We're allowed to stand there because the curtain is down and the audience can't see us. Tina said her halo really itched.

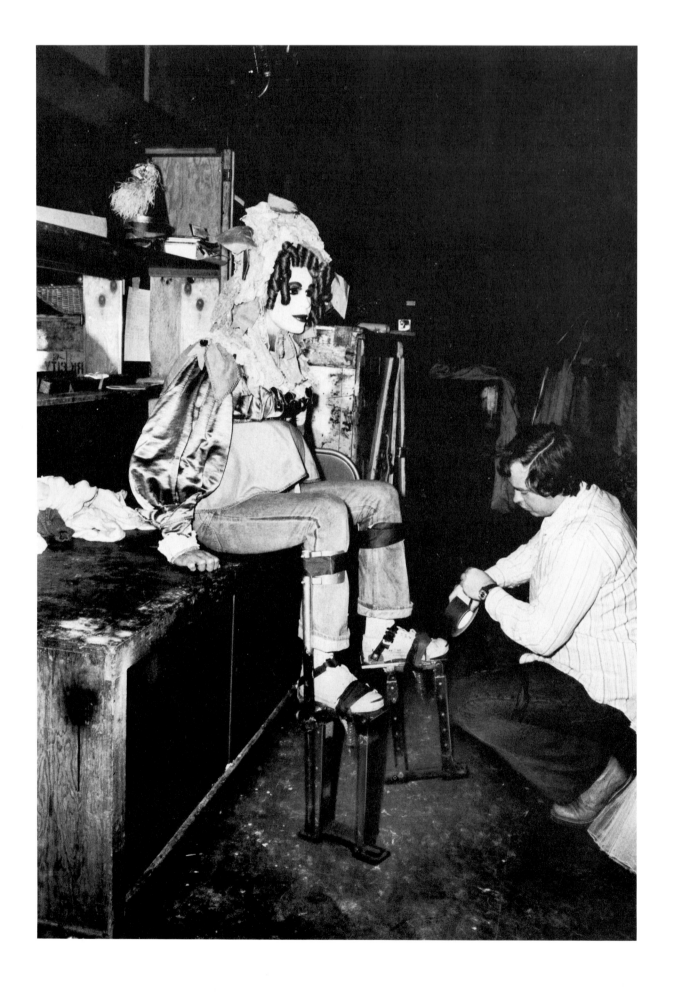

It's fun to watch Mother Ginger having her stilts strapped on before they put on her big skirt. Maybe I shouldn't say *her* skirt since Mother Ginger is always played by a man, but it sounds funny to say *his* skirt.

David was there to give us some instructions for Act II. Mainly he told the angels to remember to walk on their toes.

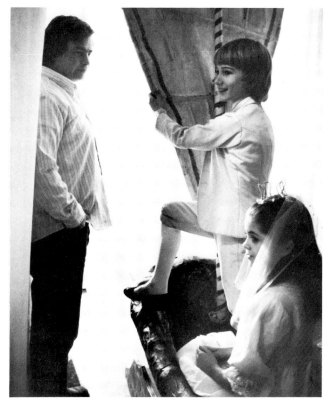

Wiley Crockett told us it was time to get into our little walnut-shell boat because the curtain was going up.

Mary doesn't do very much in Act II. We sail on stage and get welcomed to the Land of Sweets. And then Stephen does his big solo part where he tells in panto-mime about what happened in Act I. When he acted out the part about killing the Mouse King the audience applauded.

After that, Stephen and I sit on the big throne and watch all the dancers. Most of them are named after delicious things to eat. There's Coffee, the Candy Canes, Mother Ginger, and a Dew Drop Fairy and her flowers. There are some others too, but those are my favorites. Last year when Andrea was in *Nutcracker* she was the first Polichinelle to come out of Mother Ginger's skirt. She told me it's really hot under there. The skirt weighs forty pounds and it takes two stagehands to lift it because it's so large.

While we sat up there we talked a little and pretended to eat the delicious candies. Susie Eisner told me that she and Sean used to put real candy there sometimes.

I looked out at the audience to see if I could find anybody I knew, but I couldn't really see any faces.

The pas de deux by the Sugar Plum Fairy and her Cavalier is the most fun to watch. Kay Mazzo and Richard Hoskinson danced it at our first performance.

After they finished and everyone applauded we got off our throne and said goodbye to everybody in the Land of Sweets.

And off we went in our reindeer sleigh. Stephen said it really gave him butterflies in his tummy.

As soon as we go off in the sleigh, the curtain comes down so we have to jump out of it really fast backstage and get ready for the final curtain call. Everyone who was in Act II takes a bow together, and then the soloists take separate ones.

Afterwards a lot of people came backstage to say hello. There were quite a few people I didn't know and they all asked me questions—like where I studied ballet, and how I got to be Mary. They also asked me if I could steer the bed when it was going around and around on the stage.

Anita Zahn, who was my very first ballet teacher, told me that she felt very proud.

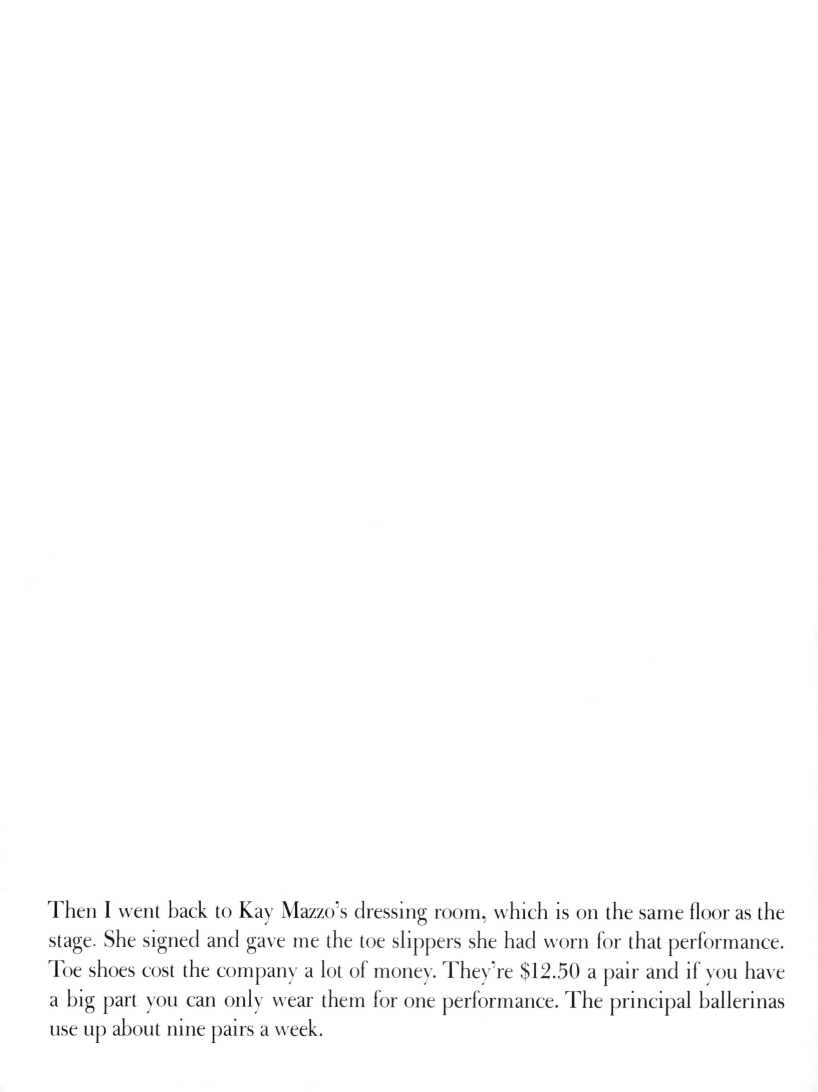

Then I went back to Kay Mazzo's dressing room, which is on the same floor as the stage. She signed and gave me the toe slippers she had worn for that performance. Toe shoes cost the company a lot of money. They're $12.50 a pair and if you have a big part you can only wear them for one performance. The principal ballerinas use up about nine pairs a week.

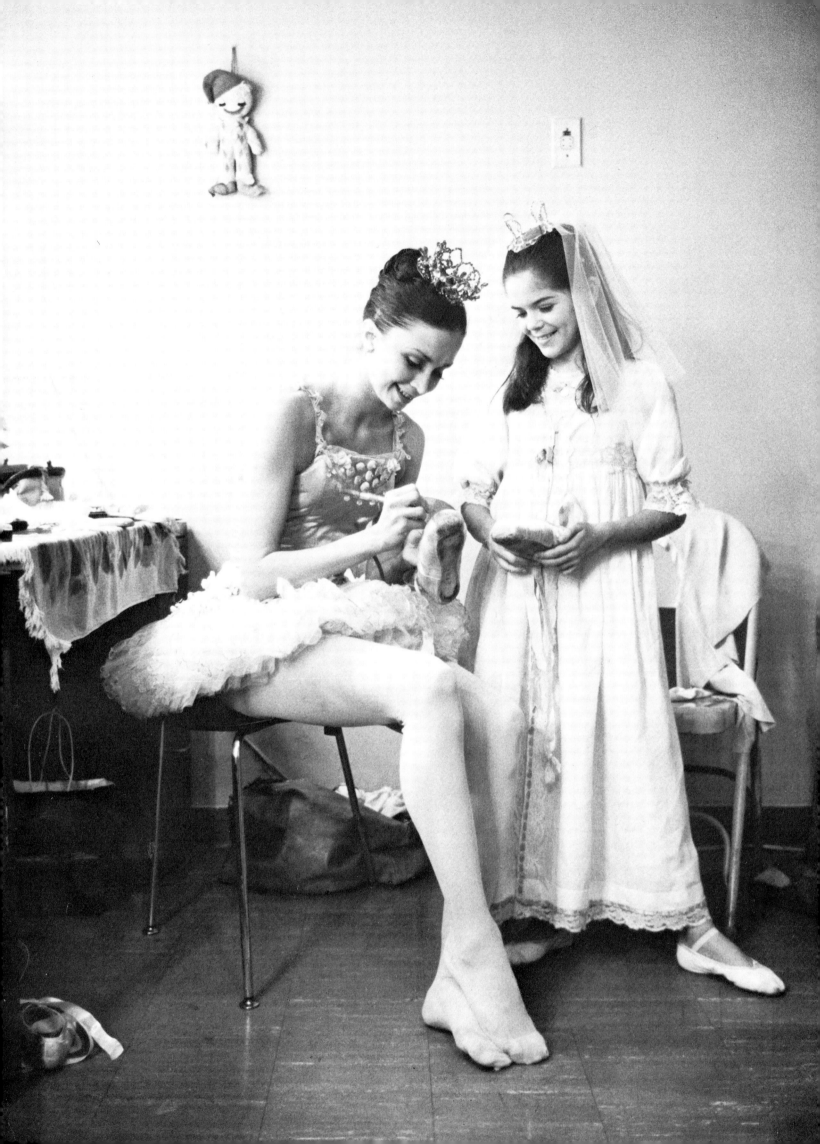

After I changed out of my costume I went outside to meet Mommy. I was the first one upstairs. People started coming by and some of them actually asked *me* for my autograph.

I didn't get to stay home very long—just long enough to have a quick dinner—because I had to be back at the theater by seven for another performance that evening. David met us backstage before the curtain went up. He told us that we had done a good job that afternoon but he had a few corrections for us. I was too excited to be tired but when I finally did get home around eleven I fell asleep before Mommy even turned out the light.

There were thirty-eight performances of *Nutcracker* and I was scheduled for nineteen of them. I watched lots of other Sugar Plum Fairies and their Cavaliers: Muriel Aasen and Daniel Duell, Suzanne Farrell with Peter Martins, Merrill Ashley and Gerald Ebitz, Patricia McBride and Jean-Pierre Bonnefous, and Colleen Neary and Peter Martins. Peter danced the role quite often. Patricia McBride and Jean-Pierre Bonnefous are married in real life so it must be fun for them to dance together. Kay danced more times too. All the Sugar Plums went to The School of American Ballet when they were younger.

On the day before Christmas, Susie Eisner hurt her foot so I got to do one extra performance. Sean Savoye was my prince. It was fun to do the extra performance because a lot of my friends were in Cast A.

Stephen also did an extra performance during the run. His brother, Michael, who plays the part of Fritz in Cast A, let Stephen do one performance for old times' sake. Stephen played Fritz for two years.

On Christmas Eve the Candy Canes all wore real candy canes on their costumes. And I gave Stephen a Christmas present.

Another exciting thing that happened was that Stephen had his birthday and we all had a party for him. He was eleven. His mother brought a cake to the theater.

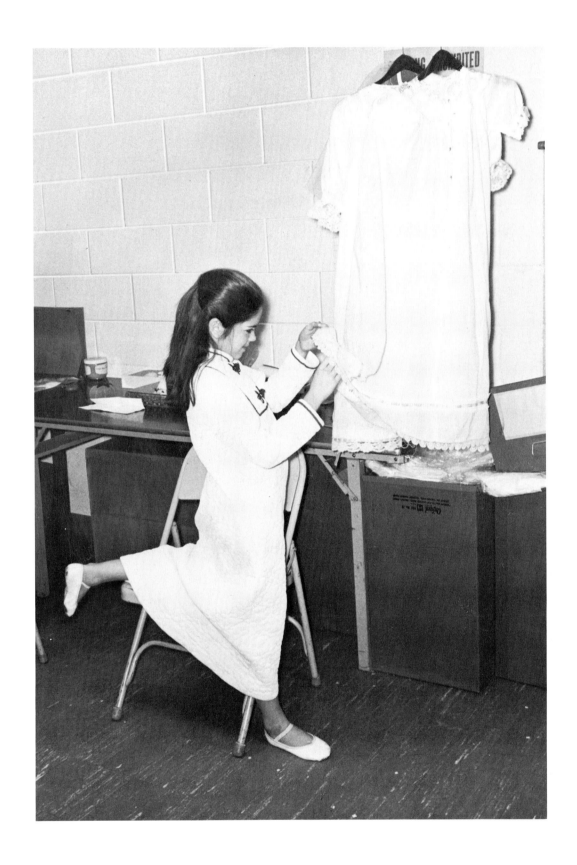

Soon it was closing night. After the last performance I tore a little pink ribbon off the pantaloons that I wore in the party scene to keep for a souvenir. Lots of the girls kissed their costumes goodbye. Tina said goodbye to her costume too. She said "Goodbye costume, I hope I'm not in you next year." I hope she'll get the party scene next time.

Tina came over to my house for dinner afterwards. We stayed up real late talking.

I hope I'll get to do Mary again. David said he's going to put me in a pickle jar so I won't grow too much and maybe I can do it again next Christmas. He's already asked me to do it in Saratoga when the company does *Nutcracker* there in July this summer. It's only for a week so I'll still have lots of time to ride my pony in Wyoming. I love dancing but I still like horses a lot too.

While *Nutcracker* was running we all had a vacation from ballet school. But as soon as it was over, I was back in class, the same as before, working on pliés and tendus. Miss Reiman was telling us to turn out and straighten our knees.

And David was <u>still</u> telling me to pull in my stomach.

Acknowledgments

There are so many people to thank. Heading the list must be Amy Robbins, for it was Amy who introduced me to The School of American Ballet. A student there herself, she is the veteran of many *Nutcrackers*, and when I asked her if I might take some pictures of her dancing she suggested I call someone at the School for permission. Fortunately, the person who answered the phone was Mary Porter, Lincoln Kirstein's assistant, and it was Mary who arranged for me to meet Natasha Gleboff, the School's Associate Director. I went over to the Juilliard building that same afternoon and felt as though I had walked into a Degas painting. I knew within minutes that I wanted to do a book, and before leaving I asked Mrs. Gleboff if it would be possible. She at once began to pave the way, introducing me to the various teachers so that I might observe their classes. The entire staff at the School was exceedingly cooperative, especially Edith Hogsett, Mary Cornell, Doreen Carrigan, and Elise Reiman.

Certainly I could not have attempted this project without the cooperation of Lincoln Kirstein and George Balanchine. It has been one of the greatest privileges of my life to have watched them both at work.

I am deeply grateful to David Richardson, a dancer with the New York City Ballet as well as the ballet master in charge of all the children. David not only let me photograph the classes he taught but allowed me to follow the auditions and all the rehearsals for *Nutcracker*. As we moved toward production he helped by introducing me to the members of the company. Long after the curtain went down on the final performance of *Nutcracker*, David continued to answer my questions while I was working on the text.

Another person who deserves special thanks is Edward Bigelow, Assistant Manager of the company, who tried, and is still trying, to teach me about ballet and what makes a ballet dancer good. He helped in every possible way through every possible crisis.

Everyone connected with the New York City Ballet was wonderful to me, particularly the dancers. And I am indebted to Virginia Donaldson and Larry Strichman of the Press Department; Barbara Horgan and Carole Deschamps of the Administrative Staff; Ronnie Bates, Kevin Tyler, and Roland Vasquez of the Technical Staff, and all the members of the crew who were always helpful when I was working backstage.

John Loengard, Picture Editor of *Life* Magazine, arranged for me to borrow some invaluable equipment from the Time-Life photo lab; Erika Leone printed the photographs; my assistant June Makela kept everything organized, and my friend Genevieve Young gave me constant and invaluable advice.

One of the nicest things that happened was having Knopf for my publisher, and even nicer was having that balletomaniac, Bob Gottlieb, for my editor, poring over contact sheets and working closely with me from beginning to end. Everyone at Knopf was a pleasure to work with: Robert Scudellari, who designed this book, Bill Loverd, Jane Becker Friedman, Lee Goerner, Nina Bourne, Anne McCormick, Ellen McNeilly, Marylea O'Reilly, Neal Jones, Elissa Ichiyasu, and especially Martha Kaplan, who held me (and the book) together.

I would also like to thank my own family—my sister, Christie Graham, my brother, Tony Kent, who is a gifted photographer now living in Paris, and my parents. They have given me the best kind of moral support.

One of my most moving experiences while I was working on *A Very Young Dancer* was taking my mother to *The Nutcracker*, for it was she who many years ago first took me to see this magical ballet. I remember two things: my astonishment as the tree began to grow, and my wonder at *how* all those children got to be up on that splendid stage. I hope this book will help to answer that question for all those who are still wondering.

In closing I would like to thank Stephanie and her family, especially her sister Andrea, and Stephen Austin, Tina Hedges, and all the children at The School of American Ballet, for this book is their book.

—Jill Krementz